FOUR STAR
SIGHT READING AND EAR TESTS

Book 7

DAILY EXERCISES FOR PIANO STUDENTS

BY BORIS BERLIN

Revised Edition

Recommended for use in conjunction with the piano examinations of the
Royal Conservatory of Music

MOZART SCHOOL OF MUSIC®

Unit 150B 6540 Burlington Avenue
Burnaby BC V5H 3M7
(604) 777 – 1808

ISBN 0-88797-215-2

PREFACE

To be able to read at sight is of the first importance to every piano student. And yet so many of them seem to have trouble, with the result that they do not make the progress they should and often lose much of the real joy of being able to play the piano.

Why do they have trouble ?

The main reason is that so very few of them practise reading at sight in any regular and systematic manner. They have an idea—a completely false idea—that reading at sight is a special gift peculiar to rarely endowed students.

Good sight reading is not difficult for any student. It is simply the result of careful preparation and regular use, through daily practice, of the powers of concentration and observation.

Of course there are some students who can read at sight better than others, or who learn to read at sight more quickly and more accurately than others. But these students, too, need regular practice if they want to develop and improve an ability without which no one can acquire true musicianship.

INTRODUCTION

While good sight reading is obviously essential to a would-be professional musician, it is no less important to the amateur. Indeed it stands to reason that, when a student has given up the idea of a musical career (if he ever entertained it), his maintaining or dropping an interest in music as a hobby will depend in almost exact proportion on his ability to read at sight. If he has nothing to play but the few pieces he has learned in his days of music study and no time to practise new ones his interest will soon pall, whereas the good sight reader may keep his interest alive with almost unlimited new material, even though he never brings his playing to a stage of technical excellence fit for public performance. I would therefore remind teachers that sight reading is *not* a "side-line" for any music student: far better let him postpone an examination or two and concentrate. He will easily make up for lost time later.

It should be impressed on a pupil that a mistake once made in sight reading *is* a mistake once and for all, and too late to recall. Having prepared himself as thoroughly as possible a candidate should play steadily — not because he will deceive the examiner if he makes mistakes — but because, for practical purposes the only sight reader worthwhile is the one that keeps going. A wrong note or chord will, to be sure, count against him, but it will doubly count against him if in going back to locate or correct it he makes a break in the rhythm. If he *does* correct it, it is in any case not playing at first sight, but at second. Of course he will keep going satisfactorily only if he has learned to read a beat or more ahead of what he is playing.

SIR ERNEST MacMILLAN
—*"On the Preparation of Ear Tests"*

AIM

The AIM of this series of Graded Books is to help students acquire a fluency in sight reading, and to prepare them for the SIGHT READING and the EAR TEST part of piano examinations.

DESCRIPTION

This book contains eight sets of DAILY SIGHT READING and EAR TEST EXERCISES. Each set should be practised by the student at home in preparation for the FOUR STAR TEST, which will be given by the teacher at the music lesson.

After the last FOUR STAR TEST, the FINAL TEST is given to the student before the issue of the CERTIFICATE OF MERIT.

The student should follow the directions when practising the DAILY SIGHT READING.

Excerpts by the following composers have been used in this book:

W. Babell (1690-1723)
W.F. Bach (1710-1784)
J. Barrett (1676-1719)
M. Basch
L. Beethoven (1770-1827)
G. Blangini (1781-1841)
A. Caldara (1670-1736)
G. Conus (1862-1933)
G. Farnaby (1563-1640)
M. Gnessin (1883-1957)
A. Goedicke (1877-1957)
C. Graupner (1683-1760)
J.N. Hummel (1778-1837)
D. Kabalevsky (1904-   )

K.M. Kunz (1812-1875)
S. Maykapar (1867-1938)
F. Mendelssohn (1809-1847)
Nicolayev
H. Purcell (1659-1695)
R. Schumann (1810-1856)
I. Seiss (1840-1905)
D. Steibelt (1765-1823)
B. Stranolubsky
G.P. Telemann (1681-1767)
N. Tigranian (1856-1951)
W. Young (17th c.)
V. Ziring

DAILY SIGHT READING <small>FOR TEST</small> No. 1

①

DATE..................

This piece is in _____ time. It is in the key of _____ and has _____ sharps/flats.
Play, counting the beats.

Before Playing look at the **Clefs, Key-Signature, Time-Signature** and **Fingering**

②

DATE..................

Put an X under each appearance of the melodic pattern [♪♪♪], then play, naming the left-hand notes.
Play again, naming the right-hand notes.

KUNZ

Clap or tap the rhythm of the melody.

PLAY ONE SET EVERY DAY

DAILY SIGHT READING _{FOR TEST} No. 1

③

DATE ....

Mark all the tonic chords (I) with an X.
Play this hymn tune harmonization while singing any voice (part).

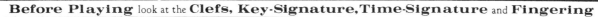

Before Playing look at the **Clefs, Key-Signature, Time-Signature** and **Fingering**

④

DATE ....

The tempo of this piece is _____ , which means _____
Trace the slurs and phrase marks and copy all the expression marks.
Play with correct expression.

SEISS

The expression marks found in this piece are: _____

PLAY ONE SET EVERY DAY

DAILY SIGHT READING FOR TEST No. 1

5 Clap or tap the rhythm of the melody.　　　　　　　　**DATE** ....

Moderato　　　　　　　　　　　　　　　　　　　　　　　W.F. BACH

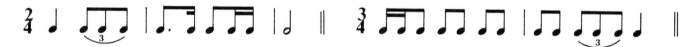

Before Playing look at the **Clefs, Key-Signature, Time-Signature** and **Fingering**

EAR TEST EXERCISES

1. Clap the rhythmic patterns (a) looking at the music; (b) from memory; or have someone clap the patterns for you to imitate.

2. Look carefully at this tune. Name the key, then clap or tap the rhythm. Play the tune
(a) looking at the music; (b) from memory.

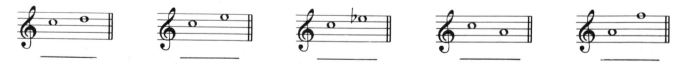

3. Play, then hum the two notes of each interval. Name the interval.

4. Play, then identify each of the following:

PLAY ONE SET EVERY DAY

★ FOUR STAR TEST No. 1 ★
AT THE LESSON WITH THE TEACHER

1. Clap or tap the rhythm of the melody.

2. Find the first note, then play without looking at the keyboard.

3. Look at these intervals. What is the difference between them? Play the intervals.

4. Play this little piece while your teacher times the reading.

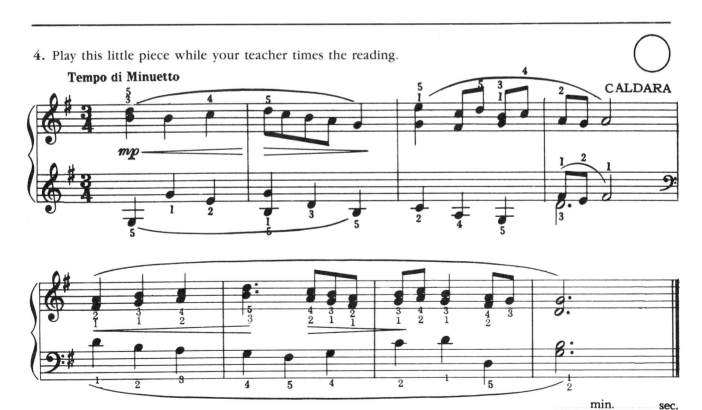

min.........sec.

FOR EAR TESTS SEE PAGES 37 and 38

DAILY SIGHT READING _{FOR TEST} No. 2

①   DATE..........................

This piece is in _____ time. It is in the key of _____ and has ____ sharps/flats.
Play, counting the beats.

GRAUPNER

Before Playing look at the **Clefs, Key-Signature, Time-Signature** and **Fingering**

②   DATE..........................

Put an X under each appearance of the rhythmic pattern ♪♩, then play, naming the left-hand notes.
Play again, naming the right-hand notes.

KUNZ

Clap or tap the rhythm of the melody.

PLAY ONE SET EVERY DAY

DAILY SIGHT READING FOR TEST No. 2

③

Mark all the dominant chords (V) with an X.
Play this Coventry Carol harmonization while singing any voice (part).

Before Playing look at the **Clefs, Key-Signature, Time-Signature** and **Fingering**

④ DATE ....

The tempo of this piece is _____ , which means _____
Trace the slurs and phrase marks and copy all the expression marks.
Play with correct expression.

The expression marks found in this piece are: _____

PLAY ONE SET EVERY DAY

DAILY SIGHT READING <small>FOR TEST</small> No. 2

(5) Clap or tap the rhythm of the melody.   DATE ....

Moderato   B.B.

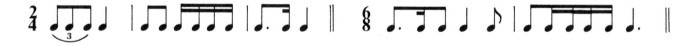

Before Playing look at the **Clefs, Key-Signature, Time-Signature** and **Fingering**

EAR TEST EXERCISES

1. Clap the rhythmic patterns (a) looking at the music; (b) from memory; or have someone clap the patterns for you to imitate.

2. Look carefully at this tune. Name the key, then clap or tap the rhythm. Play the tune (a) looking at the music; (b) from memory.

3. Play, then hum the two notes of each interval. Name the interval.

4. Play, then identify each of the following:

PLAY ONE SET EVERY DAY

★ FOUR STAR TEST No. 2 ★

AT THE LESSON WITH THE TEACHER

1. Clap or tap the rhythm of the melody.

2. Find the first note, then play without looking at the keyboard.

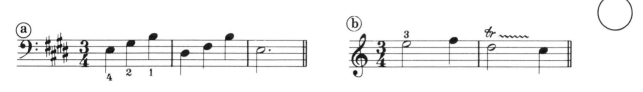

3. Look at these passages. What is the difference between them? Play both passages.

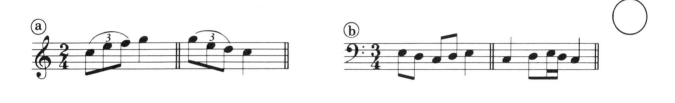

4. Play this little piece while your teacher times the reading.

.... min. .... sec.

FOR EAR TESTS SEE PAGES 37 and 38

DAILY SIGHT READING <small>FOR TEST</small> No. 3

(1)

This piece is in _____ time. It is in the key of _____ and has _____ sharps/flats.
Play, counting the beats.

Before Playing look at the **Clefs, Key-Signature, Time-Signature** and **Fingering**

(2)

Put an X under each interval of a 3rd, then play, naming the left-hand notes.
Play again, naming the right-hand notes.

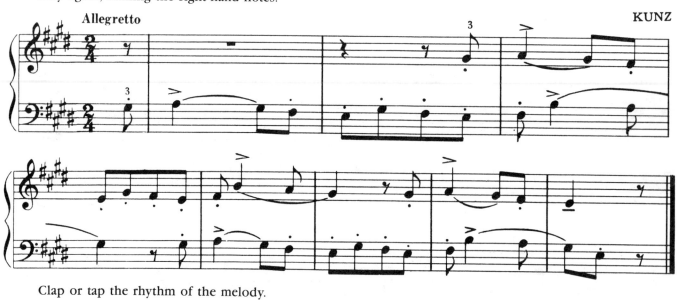

Clap or tap the rhythm of the melody.

DAILY SIGHT READING _{FOR TEST} No. 3

③   DATE ....

Mark all the subdominant chords (IV) with an X.

Play this hymn tune harmonization while singing any voice (part).

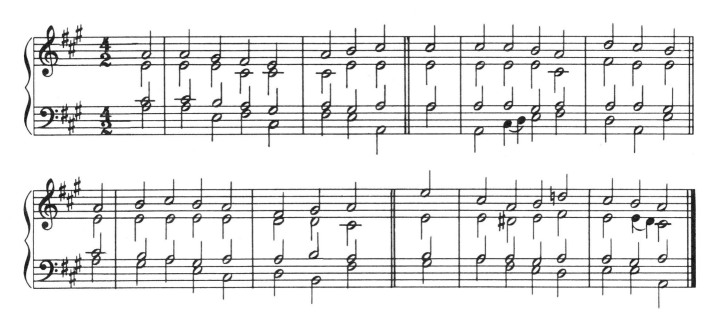

Before Playing look at the **Clefs, Key-Signature, Time-Signature** and **Fingering**

④   DATE ....

The tempo of this piece is _____ , which means _____
Trace the slurs and phrase marks and copy all the expression marks.
Play with correct expression.

The expression marks found in this piece are: _____

PLAY ONE SET EVERY DAY

DAILY SIGHT READING FOR TEST No. 3

⑤ Clap or tap the rhythm of the melody.   **DATE** ....

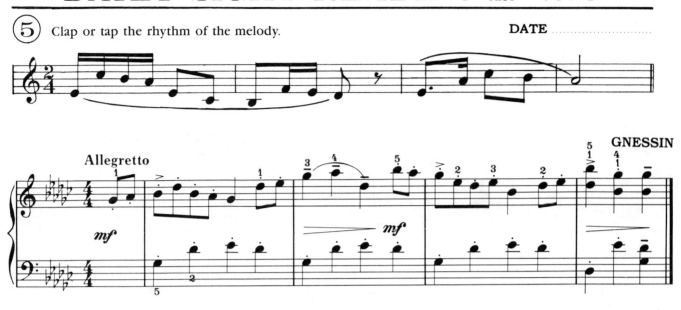

GNESSIN
Allegretto

Before Playing look at the **Clefs, Key-Signature, Time-Signature** and **Fingering**

EAR TEST EXERCISES

1. Clap the rhythmic patterns (a) looking at the music; (b) from memory; or have someone clap the patterns for you to imitate.

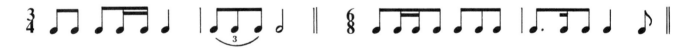

2. Look carefully at this tune. Name the key, then clap or tap the rhythm. Play the tune (a) looking at the music; (b) from memory.

3. Play, then hum the two notes of each interval. Name the interval.

4. Play, then identify each of the following:

PLAY ONE SET EVERY DAY

★ FOUR STAR TEST No. 3 ★

AT THE LESSON WITH THE TEACHER

1. Clap or tap the rhythm of the melody.

2. Find the first note, then play without looking at the keyboard.

3. Look at these notes. What is the difference between them? Play the notes.

4. Play this little piece while your teacher times the reading.

TELEMANN

min.   sec.

FOR EAR TESTS SEE PAGES 37 and 38

DAILY SIGHT READING FOR TEST No. 4

①   DATE ....

This piece is in _____ time. It is in the key of _____ and has _____ sharps/flats.
Play, counting the beats.

Smooth and in a singing style   PURCELL

Before Playing look at the **Clefs, Key-Signatures, Time Signatures** and the **Fingering**

②   DATE ....

Put an X under each E flat, then play, naming the left-hand notes.
Play again, naming the right-hand notes.

HUMMEL

Clap or tap the rhythm of the melody.

PLAY ONE SET EVERY DAY

③

Mark all the tonic chords (I) with an X.
Play this hymn tune harmonization while singing any voice (part).

④

The tempo of this piece is _____ , which means _____
Trace the slurs and phrase marks and copy all the expression marks.
Play with correct expression.

Allegretto   STEIBELT

The expression marks found in this piece are: _____

DAILY SIGHT READING <small>FOR TEST</small> No. 4

⑤ Clap or tap the rhythm of the melody.

DATE ....

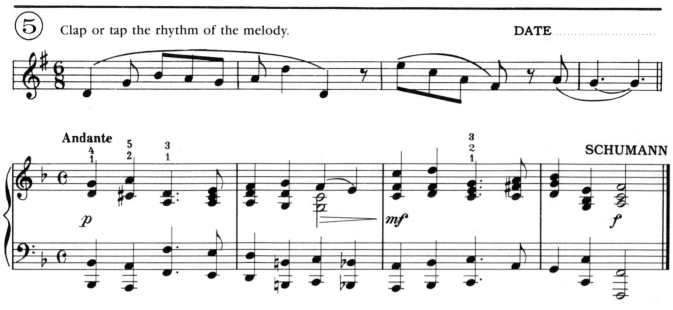

SCHUMANN

Before Playing look at the **Clefs, Key-Signature, Time-Signature** and **Fingering**

EAR TEST EXERCISES

1. Clap the rhythmic patterns of these melodies (a) looking at the music; (b) from memory; or have someone clap the patterns for you to imitate.

2. Look carefully at this tune. Name the key, then clap or tap the rhythm. Play the tune
(a) looking at the music; (b) from memory.

3. Play, then hum the two notes of each interval. Name the interval.

4. Play, then identify each of the following:

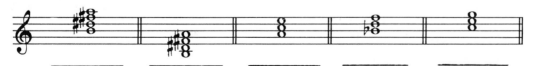

PLAY ONE SET EVERY DAY

★ FOUR STAR TEST No. 4 ★

AT THE LESSON WITH THE TEACHER

1. Clap or tap the rhythm of the melody.

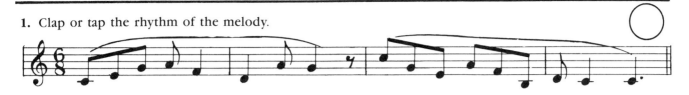

2. Find the first note, then play without looking at the keyboard.

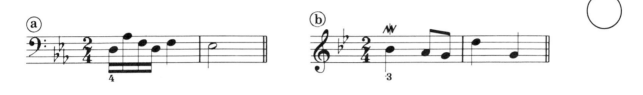

3. Look at these intervals. What is the difference between them? Play the intervals.

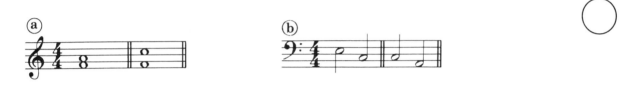

4. Play this little piece while your teacher times the reading.

min. _____ sec.

FOR EAR TESTS SEE PAGES 37 and 38

DAILY SIGHT READING FOR TEST No. 5

① DATE ....

This piece is in _____ time. It is in the key of _____ and has _____ sharps/flats.
Play, counting the beats.

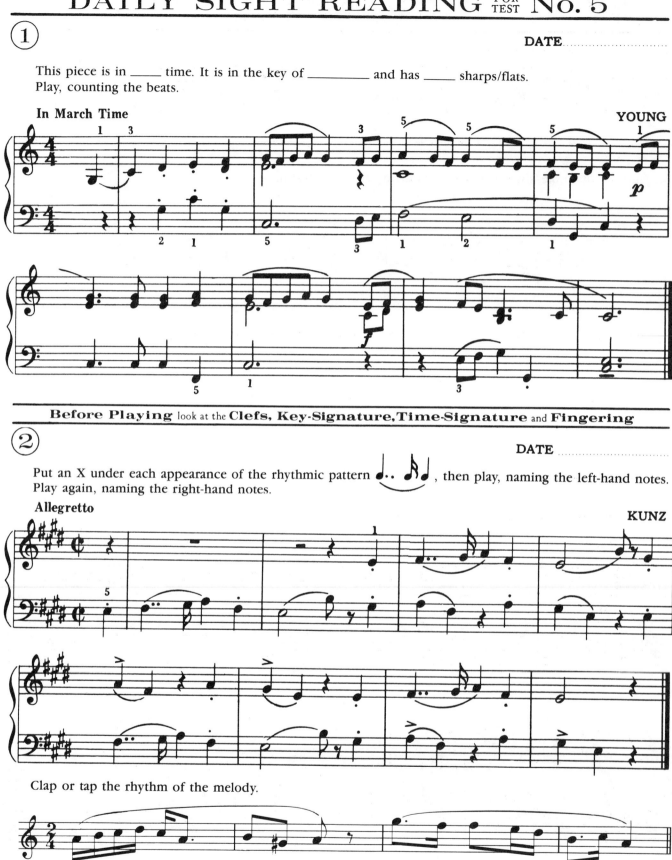

Before Playing look at the **Clefs, Key-Signature, Time-Signature** and **Fingering**

② DATE ....

Put an X under each appearance of the rhythmic pattern ♩.. ♪♩ , then play, naming the left-hand notes.
Play again, naming the right-hand notes.

Clap or tap the rhythm of the melody.

PLAY ONE SET EVERY DAY

③

Mark all the dominant chords (V) with an X.
Play this hymn tune harmonization while singing any voice (part).

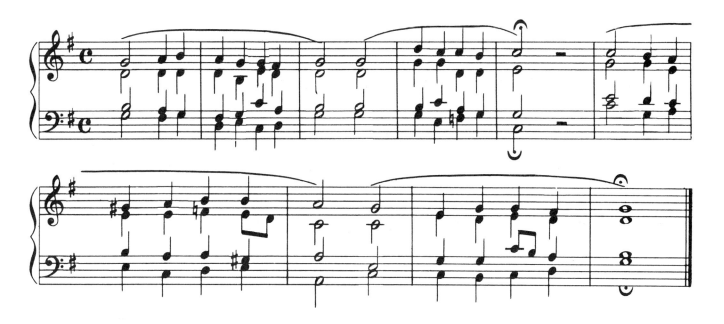

Before Playing look at the **Clefs, Key-Signature, Time-Signature** and **Fingering**

④

The tempo of this piece is _____ , which means _____
Trace the slurs and phrase marks and copy all the expression marks.
Play with correct expression.

MAYKAPAR

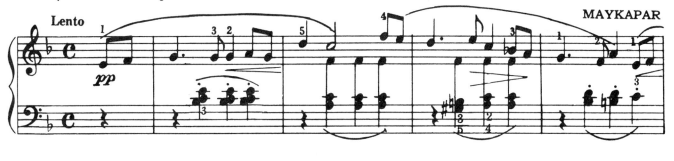

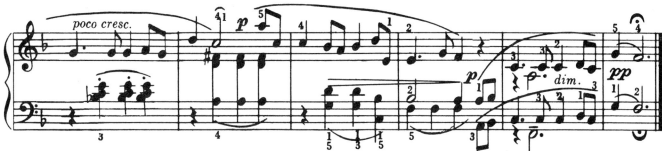

The expression marks found in this piece are: _____

PLAY ONE SET EVERY DAY

⑤ Clap or tap the rhythm of the melody.

DATE ....

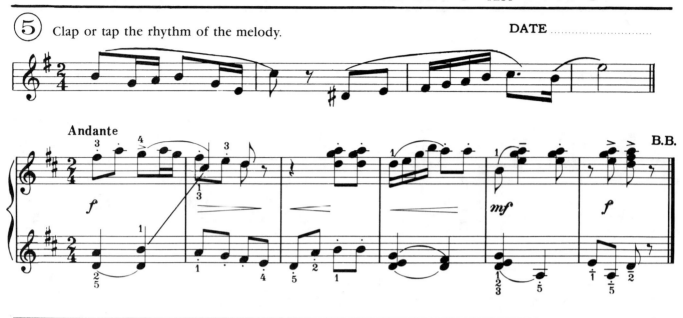

Andante

B.B.

Before Playing look at the **Clefs, Key-Signature, Time-Signature** and **Fingering**

EAR TEST EXERCISES

1. Clap the rhythmic patterns of these melodies (a) looking at the music; (b) from memory; or have someone clap the patterns for you to imitate.

2. Look carefully at this tune. Name the key, then clap or tap the rhythm. Play the tune (a) looking at the music; (b) from memory.

3. Play, then hum the two notes of each interval. Name the interval.

4. Play, then identify each of the following:

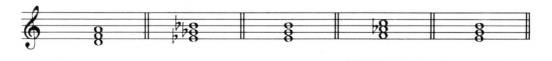

PLAY ONE SET EVERY DAY

★ FOUR STAR TEST No. 5 ★
AT THE LESSON WITH THE TEACHER

1. Clap or tap the rhythm of the melody.

2. Find the first note, then play without looking at the keyboard.

3. Look at these notes. What is the difference between them? Play the notes.

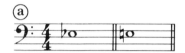

4. Play this little piece while your teacher times the reading.

Andante con moto

FARNABY

.... min. .... sec.

FOR EAR TESTS SEE PAGES 37 and 38

DAILY SIGHT READING _{FOR TEST} No. 6

(1) DATE ....

This piece is in _____ time. It is in the key of _____ and has _____ sharps/flats.
Play, counting the beats.

Before Playing look at the **Clefs, Key-Signature, Time-Signature** and **Fingering**

(2) DATE ....

Put an X under each pair of tied notes, then play, naming the left-hand notes.
Play again, naming the right-hand notes.

Clap or tap the rhythm of the melody.

PLAY ONE SET EVERY DAY

DAILY SIGHT READING <small>FOR TEST</small> No. 6

③ DATE ....

Mark all the tonic chords (I) with an X.

Play this Christmas hymn while singing any voice (part).

Before Playing look at the **Clefs, Key-Signature, Time-Signature** and **Fingering**

④ DATE ....

The tempo of this piece is _____ , which means _____

Trace the slurs and phrase marks and copy all the expression marks.

Play with correct expression.

The expression marks found in this piece are: _____

PLAY ONE SET EVERY DAY

DAILY SIGHT READING FOR TEST No. 6

⑤ Clap or tap the rhythm of the melody.   DATE.........................

Andante non troppo   ZIRING

mp espress.   dim.   p

Before Playing look at the **Clefs, Key-Signature, Time-Signature** and **Fingering**

EAR TEST EXERCISES

1. Clap the rhythmic patterns of these melodies (a) looking at the music; (b) from memory; or have someone clap the patterns for you to imitate.

2. Look carefully at this tune. Name the key, then clap or tap the rhythm. Play the tune (a) looking at the music; (b) from memory.

3. Play, then hum the two notes of each interval. Name the interval.

4. Play, then identify each of the following:

PLAY ONE SET EVERY DAY

★ FOUR STAR TEST No. 6 ★

AT THE LESSON WITH THE TEACHER

1. Clap or tap the rhythm of the melody.

2. Find the first note, then play without looking at the keyboard.

3. Look at these chords. What is the difference between them? Play the chords.

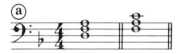 

4. Play this little piece while your teacher times the reading.

min.   sec.

FOR EAR TESTS SEE PAGES 37 and 38

DAILY SIGHT READING FOR TEST No. 7

①   DATE ....

This piece is in _____ time. It is in the key of _____ and has _____ sharps/flats.
Play, counting the beats.

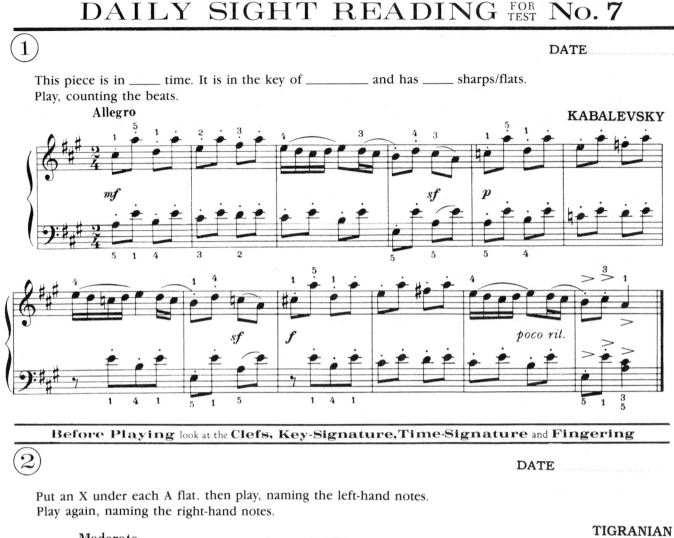

KABALEVSKY

Before Playing look at the **Clefs, Key-Signature, Time-Signature** and **Fingering**

②   DATE ....

Put an X under each A flat, then play, naming the left-hand notes.
Play again, naming the right-hand notes.

TIGRANIAN

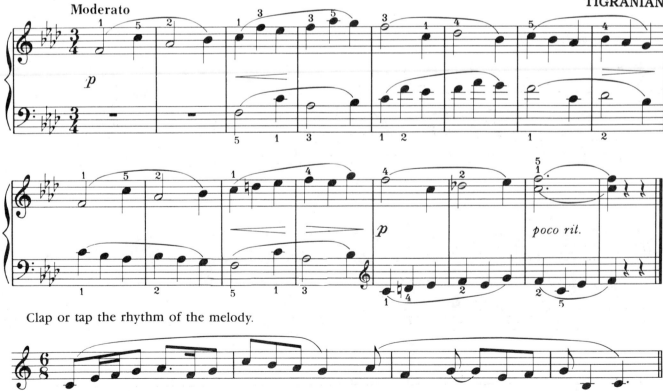

Clap or tap the rhythm of the melody.

PLAY ONE SET EVERY DAY

DAILY SIGHT READING _{FOR TEST} No.7

③

Mark all the tonic chords (I) with an X.

Play this piece while singing the melody.

Allegro non troppo

BLANGINI

Before Playing look at the **Clefs, Key-Signature, Time-Signature** and **Fingering**

④

The tempo of this piece is _____ , which means _____

Trace the slurs and phrase marks and copy all the expression marks.

Play with correct expression.

Moderato

STRANOLUBSKY

The expression marks found in this piece are: _____

PLAY ONE SET EVERY DAY

DAILY SIGHT READING FOR TEST No. 7

⑤ Clap or tap the rhythm of the melody.

DATE ....

Andante

CONUS

mp   *mf*   *f*

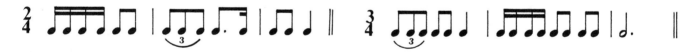

Before Playing look at the **Clefs, Key-Signature, Time-Signature** and **Fingering**

EAR TEST EXERCISES

1. Clap the rhythmic patterns (a) looking at the music; (b) from memory; or have someone clap the patterns for you to imitate.

2. Look carefully at this tune. Name the key, then clap or tap the rhythm. Play the tune (a) looking at the music; (b) from memory.

3. Play, then hum the two notes of each interval. Name the interval.

4. Play, then identify each of the following:

PLAY ONE SET EVERY DAY

★ FOUR STAR TEST No. 7 ★

AT THE LESSON WITH THE TEACHER

1. Clap or tap the rhythm of the melody.

2. Find the first note, then play without looking at the keyboard.

3. Look at these two groups of chords. What is the difference between them? Play both groups of chords.

4. Play this little piece while your teacher times the reading.

BASCH

.... min. ...... sec.

FOR EAR TESTS SEE PAGES 37 and 38

DAILY SIGHT READING <small>FOR TEST</small> No. 8

①

This piece is in _____ time. It is in the key of _____ and has _____ sharps/flats.
Play, counting the beats.

Before Playing look at the **Clefs, Key-Signature, Time-Signature** and **Fingering**

②

Put an X under each interval of a 3rd, then play, naming the left-hand notes.
Play again, naming the right-hand notes.

Clap or tap the rhythm of the melody.

PLAY ONE SET EVERY DAY

DAILY SIGHT READING <small>FOR TEST</small> No. 8

③

DATE

Mark all the tonic chords (I) with an X.
Play this piece while singing any voice (part).

Before Playing look at the **Clefs, Key-Signature, Time-Signature** and **Fingering**

④

DATE ....

The tempo of this piece is _____ , which means _____
Trace the slurs and phrase marks and copy all the expression marks.
Play with correct expression.

The expression marks found in this piece are: _____

PLAY ONE SET EVERY DAY

DAILY SIGHT READING ^{FOR TEST} No. 8

⑤ Clap or tap the rhythm of the melody.

DATE................................

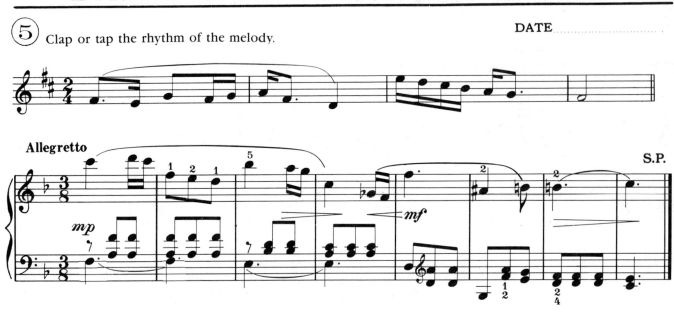

Allegretto

S.P.

mp

mf

Before Playing look at the **Clefs, Key-Signature, Time-Signature** and **Fingering**

EAR TEST EXERCISES

1. Clap the rhythmic patterns (a) looking at the music; (b) from memory; or have someone clap the patterns for you to imitate.

2. Look carefully at this tune. Name the key, then clap or tap the rhythm. Play the tune
(a) looking at the music; (b) from memory.

3. Play, then hum the two notes of each interval. Name the interval.

4. Play, then identify each of the following:

PLAY ONE SET EVERY DAY

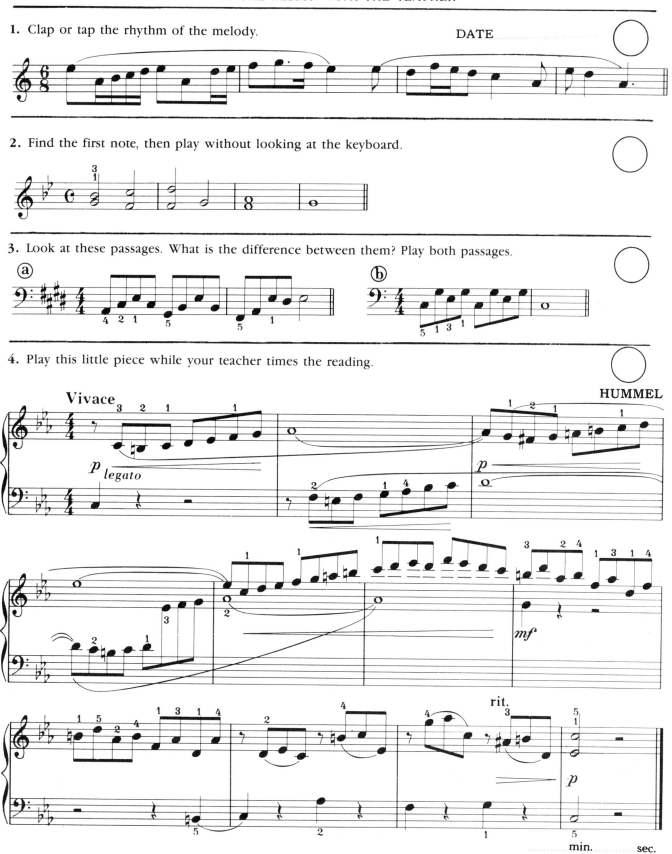

★ FOUR STAR TEST No.8 ★
AT THE LESSON WITH THE TEACHER

1. Clap or tap the rhythm of the melody.   DATE

2. Find the first note, then play without looking at the keyboard.

3. Look at these passages. What is the difference between them? Play both passages.

4. Play this little piece while your teacher times the reading.

Vivace   HUMMEL

p legato

p

mf

rit.

p

min.   sec.

FOR EAR TESTS SEE PAGES 37 and 38

★ FINAL TEST ★

This Test must be given before filling in and signing the Certificate of Merit.

① Clap or tap the rhythm of the melody.

Rating............%

② Allegro moderato

GOEDICKE

Rating............%

③ Clap or tap the rhythm of the melody.

Rating............%

④ Andante espressivo

Rating............%

Final Rating............%

EAR TESTS
AT THE LESSON WITH THE TEACHER

1. The teacher claps any of these rhythmic patterns or plays any of these melodies twice.
(The student must not see the keyboard or look at the music.)

The student then sings, taps, or claps the same rhythmic pattern from memory.

2. The teacher names the key, plays the tonic triad, then plays a melody of approximately 9 notes twice.
(The student must not see the keyboard or look at the music.)

The student must play back the same melody from memory (by ear).

3. The teacher plays the first note of any of the intervals shown below and the student then sings or hums the other note; OR

    The teacher plays the interval in broken form, and the student identifies the interval by ear. (The student must not see the keyboard or look at the music.)

    The intervals may be played in whichever octave is best suited to the range of the student's voice.

Major seconds (above a given note):

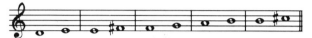

Minor seconds (above a given note):

Major thirds (above a given note):

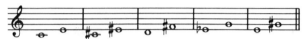

Major thirds (below a given note):

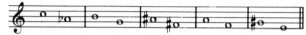

Minor thirds (above a given note):

Minor thirds (below a given note):

Major sixths (above a given note):

Minor sixths (below a given note):

Minor sixths (above a given note):

Major sevenths (below a given note):

Perfect fourths (above a given note):

Perfect fourths (below a given note):

Perfect fifths (above a given note):

Perfect fifths (below a given note):

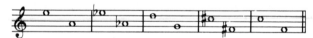

Perfect octaves (above a given note):

Perfect octaves (below a given note):

4. The teacher plays a root position major or minor triad or dominant seventh chord once only, in solid form and close position. The student must identify the chord without looking at the keyboard.

Major Triads:

Minor Triads:

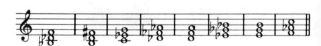

Dominant seventh chords:

Certificate of Merit

This certifies that

----

has completed

FOUR STAR SIGHT READING
Level 7

and is eligible for promotion to

FOUR STAR SIGHT READING
Level 8

Teacher . . . .

Date . . . .